HOW TO
CODE

A STEP-BY-STEP GUIDE TO
COMPUTER CODING

1 2 3 4

Book 1

Max Wainewright

Quarto
Library

INFORMATION ON RESOURCES

Here's how you can find Logo and Scratch to start coding. All these resources are free of charge.

LOGO

Logo was originally designed by Seymour Papert more than 40 years ago. There are various versions of it available.

If you are using a PC, you can download a free version of Logo from: **www.softronix.com/logo.html**

Alternatively, you can start using Logo straight away by opening up your web browser and visiting: **www.turtleacademy.com/playground/en** or **www.calormen.com/jslogo/**

SCRATCH

You can use Scratch on a PC or Mac by opening your web browser and going to: **http://scratch.mit.edu** Then click "Create" or "Try it out."

There is a very similar website called "Snap," which also works on iPads. It is available here: **http://snap.berkeley.edu/run**

If you want to run Scratch without using the web, you can download it from here: **http://scratch.mit.edu/scratch2download/**

Download our robots to use as sprites on Scratch! Go to http://www.qed-publishing.co.uk/extra-resources.php or scan this:

Internet safety

Children should be supervised when using the internet, particularly when using an unfamiliar website for the first time.
The publisher and author cannot be held responsible for the content of the websites referred to in this book.

Quarto is the authority on a wide range of topics.

Quarto educates, entertains and enriches the lives of our readers—enthusiasts and lovers of hands-on living.

www.quartoknows.com

Design and illustration: Mike Henson
Editor: Claudia Martin
Project Editor: Carly Madden
Consultant: Sean McManus
Editorial Director: Victoria Garrard
Art Director: Laura Roberts-Jensen

This library edition published in 2015 by Quarto Library., an imprint of QEB Publishing, Inc.

6 Orchard, Lake Forest, CA 92630

Distributed in the United States and Canada by Lerner Publisher Services
241 First Avenue North
Minneapolis, MN 55401 U.S.A.
www.lernerbooks.com

A CIP record for the book is available from the Library of Congress.

ISBN 978 1 93958 188 4

Printed in the United States

Scratch is developed by the Lifelong Kindergarten Group at MIT Media Lab. See http://scratch.mit.edu

For more information on Logo: www.logofoundation.org

CONTENTS :: BOOK 1

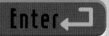

Enter ⏎

INTRODUCTION

This book is going to teach you how to code—that's another way of saying that you'll learn how to tell computers what to do. First of all, let's meet our friendly robot Ada, who is named after the world's first computer programmer: Ada Lovelace.

Meet Ada

Ada Lovelace (1815–52) was born in England 200 years ago. She worked out that a machine would be able to solve problems if it was given step-by-step instructions—a program. However, there were no computers yet for her to test her ideas on!

What is coding?

Coding means writing a set of words, or "code," that will tell a computer what to do. The words need to be written in a special language that the computer will understand. This book looks at two languages: Logo and Scratch. Coding is also called computer programming. All computers need a program to tell them what to do. Laptops, tablets, phones, and desktop computers all need programs to be useful.

Inside your computer

Input

A mouse, keyboard, and touch screen are all "input devices." They let us put information into a computer or tablet.

Output

A printer, screen, and speakers are all "output devices." Output devices are ways for a computer to tell you things.

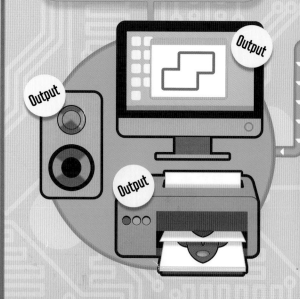

GIVING INSTRUCTIONS

There are lots of ways we can ask people to do things. If someone said "turn on the lights," "put the lights on," or even "it's dark—turn on the thingy," you would know what to do. But to program a computer, we need to give exactly the right words—and in the right order. Words that tell computers and people what to do are called instructions.

Making breakfast

Imagine you are programming our friendly robot Ada to make breakfast. Can you put these instructions in the correct order?

A Open the cereal box.

B Pour some milk onto the cereal.

C Take the lid off the milk carton.

D Pour some cereal into the bowl.

E Get a bowl from the cupboard.

Become a human robot

It's time to become a human robot! It will help you think about how to give precise instructions. You need a partner to play this game.

One of you needs to pretend to be a robot. The other one needs to be the programmer and give instructions to the robot. This player's task is to give the robot instructions to walk to the door. The only commands that can be given to the robot are:

Walk forward.

Turn left.

Turn right.

Stop.

Incorrect instruction

Incorrect instruction!

Robot artist

Here's another game to help you practice giving instructions.

You need:

1. A partner
2. A piece of paper
3. A pencil

Sit at a table next to your partner. One of you needs to be the robot artist, while the other is the programmer. The programmer needs to give the robot instructions to draw one of the pictures below. This time the robot is just moving a pencil. The robot artist is only allowed to do what the programmer says. Here are the commands you can use:

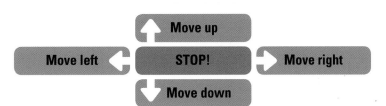

Move up
Move left
STOP!
Move right
Move down

Once you get good at this game, why not try getting the robot to play with their eyes closed. Be careful not to draw on the table!

Can you get the robot to draw anything else?

Key word

Program: Instructions that tell a computer or robot what to do.

STEP BY STEP

Computer programs need instructions to make things happen. Sometimes we need a program to solve a particular problem. To solve that problem, we need to plan the steps the program will need to take—we call the steps an algorithm.

Take a journey

Here is your problem: Ada needs to travel from square number 3 to square number 4. Work out the steps she will need to take.

To travel from **3** to **4** Ada needs to take the following steps:

↑ UP → RIGHT ↑ UP → RIGHT → RIGHT ↓ DOWN → RIGHT

Using the grid on the next page, start at **1** and take the following steps.
Where do you end up? Turn to page 30 for the answer.

↓ DOWN ↓ DOWN ↓ DOWN ↓ DOWN ↓ DOWN LEFT ←

If you want, you could write down letters instead of drawing arrows.
For example, you could write **right, right, up, down** as **R R U D**.

1. Write down an algorithm that explains how to get from **6** to **1**
2. Now try to get from **5** to **6**
3. Travel from **2** to **4**

Now check your answers on page 30.

Turn to page 30 for the answer.

Key word

Algorithm: The steps a program needs to take in order to solve a problem.

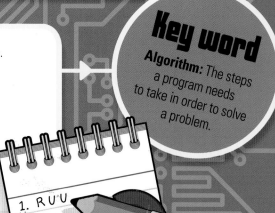

1. R U U
2.

Amazing algorithms game

For this game, you'll need a die and a small object to use as a counter.

1 Throw the die once. Put your counter on the number you threw.

2 Throw the die again (if you get the same number, throw again).

3 This is the number you need to get to.

4 Write down the steps you need to take to get there.

Use a coin or a toy person as a counter.

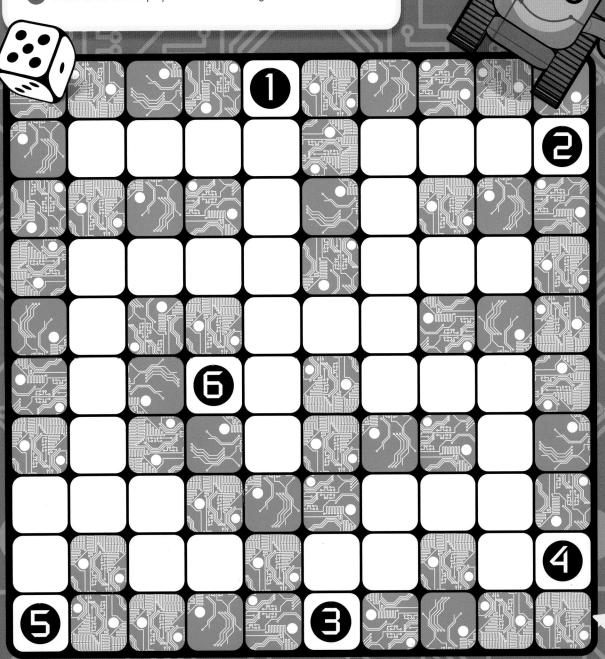

CODED MESSAGES

Giving commands

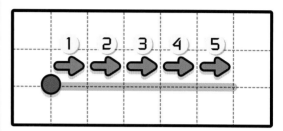

R5 means move right 5 squares. The red circle tells you where to start.

We're going to make our instructions more useful by using numbers to show how far we need to move in each direction. Special instructions like this are called commands.

Example commands

U4 means: Move up 4.
L3 means: Move left 3.
D7 means: Move down 7.
R4 means: Move right 4.

Let's see what **R3 U3 L3 D3** will draw. You need to start at the red circle:

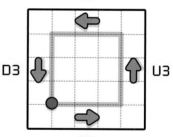

L3

D3   U3

R3

Oops! That was too far.

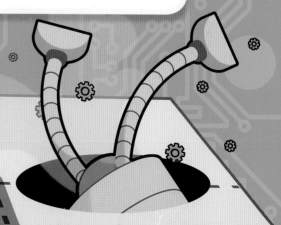

Word game

Now try writing down the commands that will spell out these words:

There's more than one right answer for some of these!

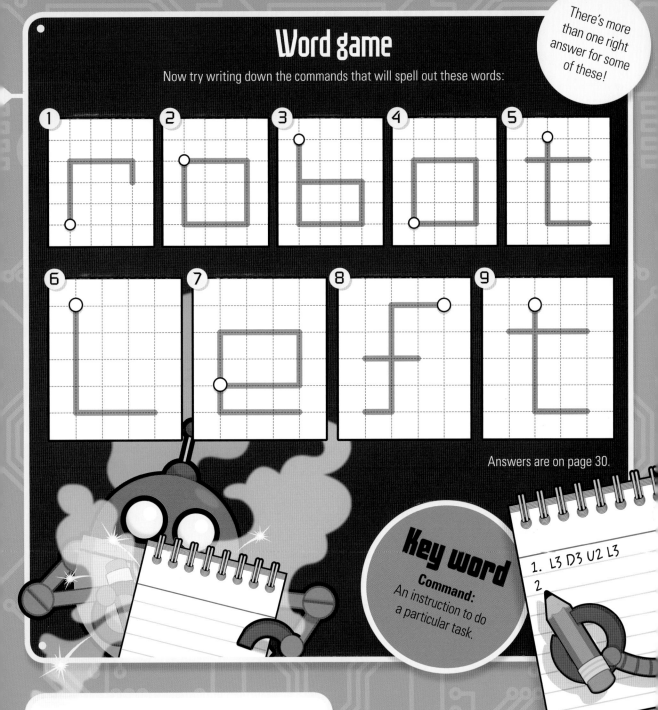

Answers are on page 30.

Key word

Command: An instruction to do a particular task.

1. L3 D3 U2 L3
2

You name it!

Try to write down the commands to spell out your name or initials. You'll need graph paper and a pencil.

1. Draw your name on graph paper. You'll have to turn diagonals (like in V, W, or M) into horizontal and vertical lines!

2. Write down the commands to draw your letters.

3. Give the commands to a partner to see if he or she can follow them.

11

SPINNING AROUND

Now we're going to learn how to make a robot move around. We need to use three commands: move forward, turn left, or turn right—and by how much.

Get to grips with degrees

The amount that robots turn is measured in degrees. Degrees can be hard to understand, but figuring out the basics will allow you to make your robot turn. A right angle is 90 degrees. A complete turn around is 360 degrees. Basically, the bigger the number, the bigger the turn.

Degrees are measured from 0 to 360. A turn of 360 degrees makes a full circle.

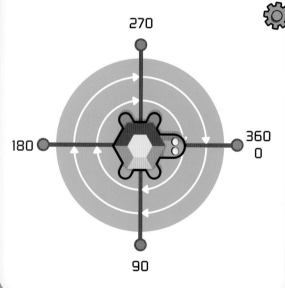

Here are examples of simple commands to make your robot turtle turn right and left:

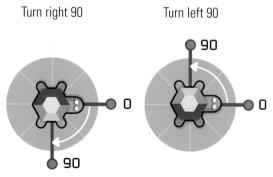

Turn right 90

Turn left 90

Tell it to turn

We're going to try this program:

Forward 25
Right 90
Forward 20
Right 90
Forward 25
Left 90
Forward 10

If you're having trouble working out lefts and rights, try turning this page around to face the same way as the turtle.

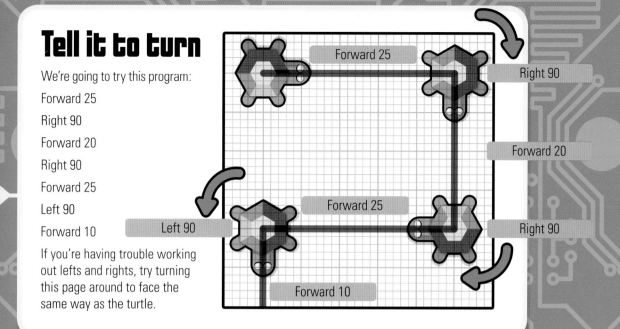

Forward 25
Right 90
Forward 20
Right 90
Forward 25
Left 90
Forward 10

Writing letters

Now try to work out what instructions will make these letters.
Check your answers on page 30.

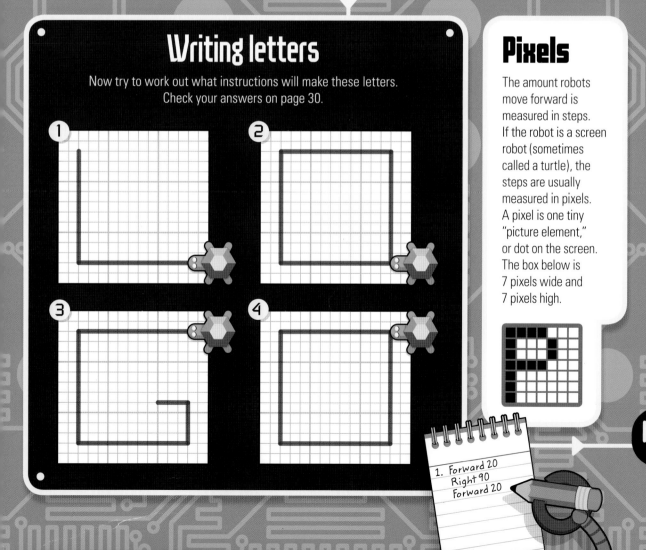

① ② ③ ④

1. Forward 20
   Right 90
   Forward 20

Pixels

The amount robots move forward is measured in steps. If the robot is a screen robot (sometimes called a turtle), the steps are usually measured in pixels. A pixel is one tiny "picture element," or dot on the screen. The box below is 7 pixels wide and 7 pixels high.

LEARNING LOGO

We're going to learn how to program in Logo, which is one of the simplest computer languages. Using Logo is a great way to put some basic commands into action!

The Logo screen

Before we start learning some commands, let's look at what we will see on the Logo screen. In the example below, we've already typed three commands into the command box. You can press **"Enter"** after each command—or type a series of commands separated by spaces, then press **"Enter"** to see the result.

Each version of Logo is slightly different. Some have **"Run"** buttons and some don't.
If your version doesn't, then press **"Enter"** after typing a command.

If there is only a thin command box, type commands one at a time, then press **"Enter,"** or click **"Run"** to run them one at a time. Alternatively, type several commands in a line with a space between each command, then press **"Enter"** or click **"Run"** to test them all.

This is the drawing box.

This is the command box. Type your program here.

Click **"Run"** to test your code or press the **"Enter"** key.

Turn to page 2 for help with downloading Logo or finding a website where you can use it.

Run

fd 50
rt 90
fd 50

fd = forward
rt = right
lt = left

Basic commands

1

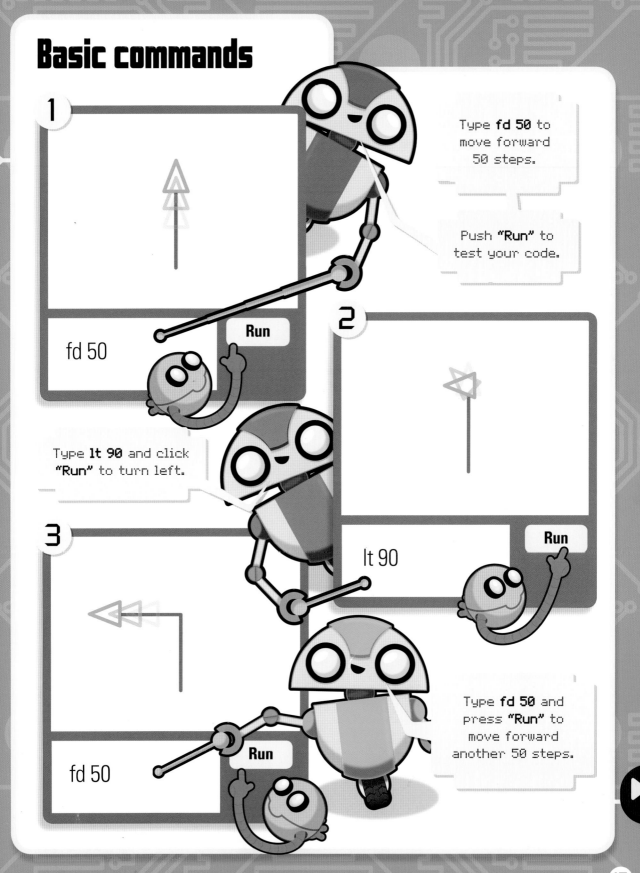

fd 50

Run

Type **fd 50** to move forward 50 steps.

Push **"Run"** to test your code.

2

lt 90

Run

Type **lt 90** and click **"Run"** to turn left.

3

fd 50

Run

Type **fd 50** and press **"Run"** to move forward another 50 steps.

LOGO SHAPES

Get in shape

Type in these programs to practice coding with Logo:

```
fd 60
rt 90
fd 60
rt 90
fd 60
rt 90
fd 60
```

Now you understand how Logo works, try drawing different shapes. Experiment with what you can create— now you're doing some great coding!

Type **cs** when you need to clear the screen.

```
fd 50
lt 90
fd 100
lt 90
fd 50
lt 90
fd 100
```

```
fd 100
rt 90
fd 50
lt 90
lt 90
fd 100
```

```
fd 25
rt 90
fd 25
lt 90
fd 25
rt 90
fd 25
```

lt 90 means turn left 90 degrees.

Type **seth 0** to make the turtle point up again.

Now spend some time experimenting. See what you can draw with Logo!

16

Try these

What do these programs draw?

1
```
lt 90
fd 50
rt 90
fd 100
rt 90
fd 50
```

2
```
fd 100
rt 90
fd 100
rt 90
fd 100
rt 90
fd 100
```

3
```
fd 50
rt 90
fd 50
lt 90
fd 50
rt 90
fd 50
rt 90
fd 100
rt 90
fd 100
```

Super Computer 7000

Shape up!

Now try to draw these shapes using Logo:

4

5

6

7

Amazing!

Ooooo!

Aaahh!

See page 30 for suggested answers.
There is more than one right answer!

17

STARTING SCRATCH

Scratch uses a similar approach to Logo, making a turtle (or sprite) move around the screen.

The Scratch screen

First of all, let's get used to the basic idea of how Scratch works. In Scratch you drag and join your commands together instead of typing them. Start by going to the Scratch website.

For help finding Scratch and similar programs turn to page 2.

Click **"Create"** or **"Try it out."** Your screen should look like the one below.

TRY IT OUT

Choose the group of commands from here.

File▼ Edit▼ Tips About

Scripts | Costumes | Sounds

Motion   Events
Looks   Control
Sound   Sensing
Pen   Operators
Data   More Blocks

Move 10 steps

Turn ↻ 15 degrees

Turn ↺ 15 degrees

Pen down
Move 10 steps
Turn ↻ 10 degre
Move 80 steps

I am the sprite that obeys your commands.

This area is called the stage. This is where you can watch your sprite moving about.

These are the commands in the current group.

This is the scripts area—drag your commands over here. If you need to remove a command, just drag it off the scripts area.

How to make a simple program

1 Choose the **Motion** group of commands. Drag a **"Move 10 steps"** command block to the scripts area.

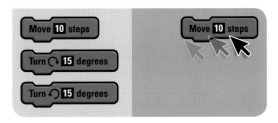

2 Click it!

On the stage, the cat sprite should move 10 steps.

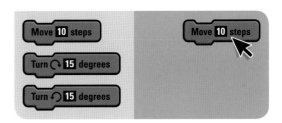

3 Change your code to **"Move 20 steps,"** by clicking in the box and typing "20."

Click it to test it.

4 Drag a **"Turn 15 degrees"** code block to join it.

Click to test your code.

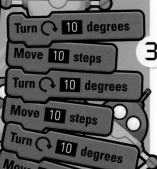

Experiment by changing the amount to move and turn.

5 You can drag several code blocks together to make a program!

Click any block to run the whole program.

PEN DOWN

Now let's learn how to draw using Scratch. We need to use the command "Pen down," then command the sprite to move around.

All square

Try this exercise to draw a square:

1

Click on the **Pen** group.

Looks	Control
Sound	Sensing
Pen	Operators
Data	More Blocks

2

Drag **"Pen down"** to the scripts area.

3

Click on the **Motion** group.

Motion	Events
Looks	Control
Sound	Sensing

4

Drag a **"Move 10 steps"** code block to join your program.

Move **10** steps

Pen down
Move **10** steps

5

Change the 10 to 60.

Pen down
Move **60** steps

6

Complete the program:

Pen down
Move **60** steps
Turn ↻ **90** degrees
Move **60** steps
Turn ↻ **90** degrees
Move **60** steps
Turn ↻ **90** degrees
Move **60** steps

Click any block to run the program.

20

Drawing shapes

Now change your code so it looks like this:

```
Pen down
Move 20 steps
Turn ↻ 90 degrees
Move 80 steps
Turn ↻ 90 degrees
Move 20 steps
Turn ↻ 90 degrees
Move 80 steps
```

Try to guess what your code will draw. Then click the first command to run your code.

Do not panic! Do not PANIC!!

Storing your work

Click the **File** menu at the top of the screen on the left. Then click:
New—to start some new work.
Download to your computer—to save a file onto your computer.
Upload from your computer—to open a file you have saved earlier.

More shapes!

Now try to draw these shapes using Scratch:

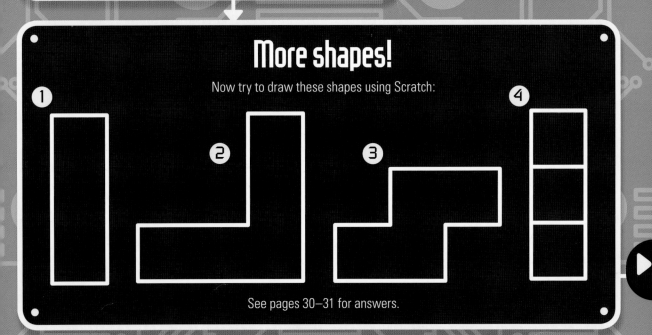

1️⃣ 2️⃣ 3️⃣ 4️⃣

See pages 30–31 for answers.

PRESS A KEY

So far, all the code we have written runs when we tell it to start. We are now going to learn how to make our code change when different keys are pressed. A key pressed during a program is a type of input.

Right and left

When **"R"** is pressed, we want the sprite to move right. When **"L"** is pressed, we want it to move left.

Press R to move right

1

Browser

scratch.mit.edu

Start Scratch. Click **"Create"** or **"Try it out."**

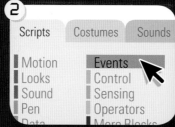

2

| Scripts | Costumes | Sounds |

Motion   Events
Looks   Control
Sound   Sensing
Pen   Operators
Data   More Blocks

Click on the **Events** group.

3

when space ▼ key pressed

Drag **"When key pressed"** to the scripts area.

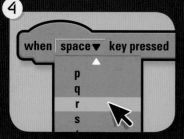

4

when space ▼ key pressed

p
q
r
s

Select **"r"** as your key.

5

| Scripts | Costumes | Sounds |

Motion   Events
Looks   Control
Sound   Sensing
Pen   Operators
Data   More Blocks

Click on the **Motion** group.

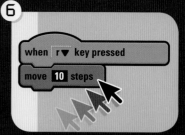

6

when r ▼ key pressed

move 10 steps

Drag **"Move steps"** to the scripts area.

Now try pressing the R key on the keyboard . . .

Press L to move left

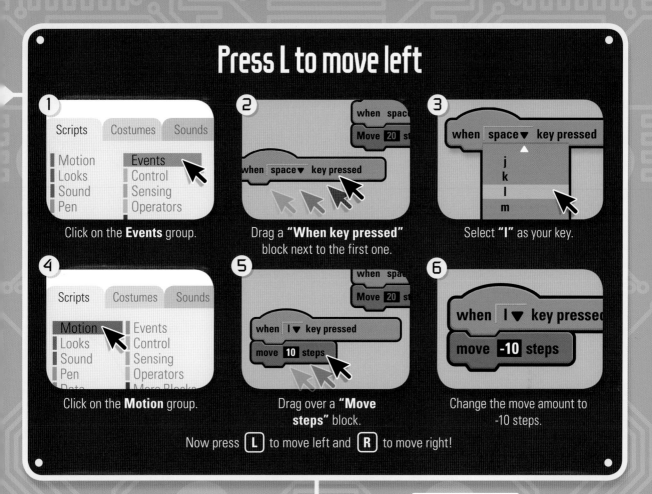

1 Click on the **Events** group.

2 Drag a **"When key pressed"** block next to the first one.

3 Select **"l"** as your key.

4 Click on the **Motion** group.

5 Drag over a **"Move steps"** block.

6 Change the move amount to -10 steps.

Now press **L** to move left and **R** to move right!

How does the code work?

We have made two different pieces of code. When we press the **"R"** key on the keyboard, this tells Scratch to move the sprite right by 10 steps.

When we press the **"L"** key, it tells Scratch to move the sprite by minus 10 steps—making it move in the opposite direction by 10 steps.

Each piece of code runs when we press a key. We are using two different inputs to make our program run two different lines of code.

Can you make your sprite move more quickly?

Change your code so the sprite will move when you press the arrow keys on the keyboard.

Key word
Input: An action (such as pressing a key) that tells a program to do something.

INPUTS AND DIRECTIONS

We've learned how to move a sprite to the right and left. We will now find out how to move it up, down, and any other direction you want by pressing different keys.

Using degrees to make turns

We are going to make a program that has four different input keys. Each input key will run code that makes the sprite point in a different direction.

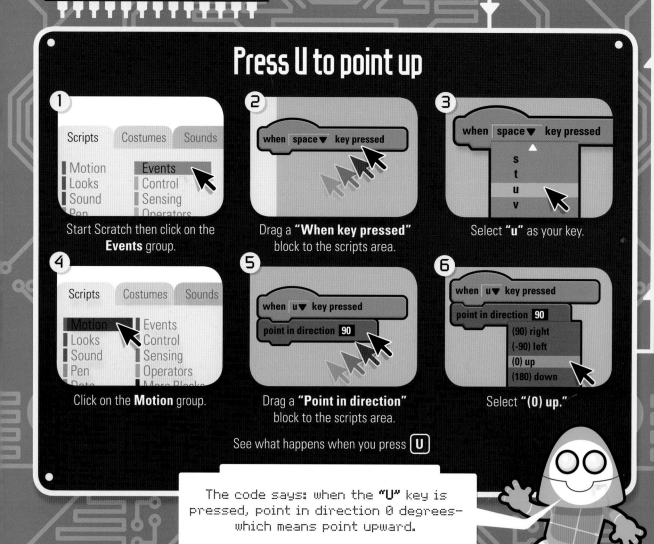

Press U to point up

1

Scripts	Costumes	Sounds
Motion	Events	
Looks	Control	
Sound	Sensing	
Pen	Operators	

Start Scratch then click on the **Events** group.

2

when space ▼ key pressed

Drag a **"When key pressed"** block to the scripts area.

3

when space ▼ key pressed

s
t
u
v

Select **"u"** as your key.

4

Scripts	Costumes	Sounds
Motion	Events	
Looks	Control	
Sound	Sensing	
Pen	Operators	
Data	More Blocks	

Click on the **Motion** group.

5

when u ▼ key pressed
point in direction 90

Drag a **"Point in direction"** block to the scripts area.

See what happens when you press Ⓤ

6

when u ▼ key pressed
point in direction 90

(90) right
(-90) left
(0) up
(180) down

Select **"(0) up."**

The code says: when the "U" key is pressed, point in direction 0 degrees— which means point upward.

24

Press D to point down

We still need to make the sprite move. When we press **"D,"** we want it to point down.

1

Drag in a **"Move steps"** block. Press U to test it!

2

Drag over another **"When key pressed"** block. Put it next to the first one.

3

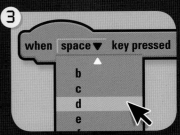

This time, select **"d"** as your key.

4

Drag in a **"Point in direction"** block.

5

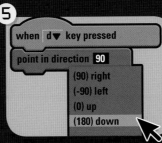

Select **"(180) down."**

6

Drag in another **"Move steps"** block.

Check your code works by pressing U and D

You need to finish this program by adding code to make the sprite move left and right. Add two more **"When key pressed"** blocks, so they change the sprite's direction when **"L"** and **"R"** are pressed.

Point **left** and move:

Point **right** and move:

Woohoo!

SKETCHING WITH INPUTS

Create your own drawing game

Now that we know how to move a sprite around with input commands, we are going to make a simple sketching program. Players will be able to draw what they want by pressing different keys to paint up, down, left, or right.

1

Start Scratch, then make a program that will move the sprite up, down, left, and right. Turn back to page 24 for a reminder of how to do this.

Test your program!

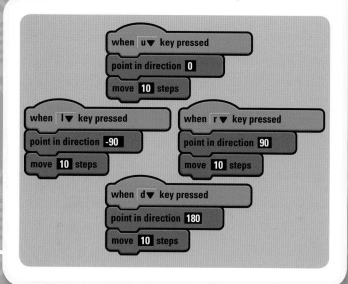

Challenge

Try changing the keys used to move things around. You could use the cursor (arrow) keys.

2

We need to make the sprite draw a line when it moves. Click on the **Pen** group. Drag a **"Pen down"** block onto the scripts area. Click the **"Pen down"** block, then try pressing the **U**, **D**, **R**, and **L** keys.

3

To clear the screen we need to use the **"Clear"** command block. Drag it over to the scripts area then try clicking it.

4

Join the **"Clear"** and **"Pen down"** blocks together.

Click on the **Events** group. Drag over a **"When green flag clicked"** block and put it above the **"Clear"** and **"Pen down"** blocks.

Now the sprite will be ready to draw a new picture whenever the green flag is clicked.

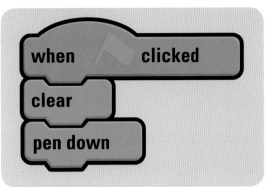

```
when [green flag] clicked
clear
pen down
```

5

The large sprite can get in the way when drawing.

Shrink it using this icon.

Click the icon then click on the sprite to make it smaller.

Scripts

Your program is now complete! Click the green flag icon to start using it to draw.

Computers use numbers to represent colors. Scratch uses numbers between 0 and 199. Some other computer languages use up to 16 million different colors!

Do you like my new sweater? I wanted something that was in shade 15,999,999!

Challenge

Can you add some commands that will let players change the pen color? You will need to use **"When key pressed"** blocks from the **Events** group, and **"Set pen color to"** blocks from the **Pen** group.

```
when [g ▼] key pressed
set pen color to 50
```

You will need to add a **"When key pressed"** block and **"Set pen color to"** block for each color you want to use. Experiment with different numbers and keep testing your code.

DEBUGGING

Coding can be a process of trial and error—testing out ideas and seeing if they work. It is common to make mistakes when doing this. A bug is another name for a mistake in a piece of code that stops it working properly. Debugging means fixing those mistakes. You'll find the answers to these questions on page 30.

1 Bugs for breakfast

Get started with debugging by finding the mistake in these instructions for making a piece of toast:

1 Get a piece of bread.

2 Put it in the toaster.

3 Spread butter on the toast.

4 Take the toast out of the toaster.

2 B wrong

Here are some commands to draw a letter b, like the one shown here. But what's wrong with the commands?

Start at the circle.
D4 R3 D2 L3

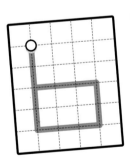

3 Logo bug

This rectangle is 100 pixels high and 300 pixels wide.

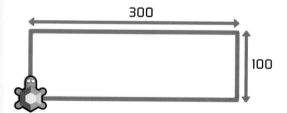

300

100

This code should draw the rectangle—but there's a bug or two somewhere!

```
fd 100
rt 90
fd 300
righrtt 90
fd 100
rt 90
fd 90
```

4 Scratch bug

Here is some Scratch code to draw a square.
The square should be 200 pixels by 200 pixels.

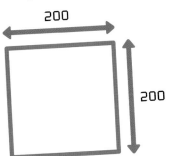

Find the bug in the code:

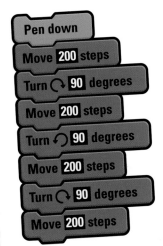

5 Broken game

This Scratch program should make a sprite do two things:

Move **up** when Ⓤ is pressed.

```
when u ▼ key pressed
point in direction 0
move 10 steps
```

Move **down** when Ⓓ is pressed.

Find the bug in the code.

```
when d ▼ key pressed
point in direction 90
move 10 steps
```

Key word

Debugging: Getting rid of mistakes that stop your code from working properly.

> Here are some tips to help you when you're debugging.

Debugging tips

When your code doesn't do what you want it to:

1. Go through your code step by step, thinking about what each command does.
2. Draw a picture or diagram to help you.
3. Have a break for a few minutes!

Think about these guidelines when you are coding:

1. Plan your program carefully first, either with a diagram or some written notes.
2. When you are learning to code, it is better to write lots of small, simple programs rather than one larger and more complex program.
3. Test your program as you are building it—don't wait until you have put in all the commands.

ANSWERS

1.
2.
3.

4	**5**	**6**	**7**
fd 100	fd 80	fd 100	fd 30
rt 90	lt 90	rt 90	rt 90
fd 100	fd 40	fd 100	fd 30
rt 90	rt 90	rt 90	lt 90
fd 100	fd 20	fd 100	fd 30
rt 90	rt 90	rt 90	rt 90
fd 100	fd 100	fd 100	fd 30
rt 180	rt 90	rt 90	lt 90
fd 50	fd 20	fd 50	fd 30
lt 90	rt 90	rt 90	rt 90
fd 100	fd 40	fd 100	fd 30
	lt 90	rt 90	lt 90
	fd 80	fd 50	fd 30
	rt 90	rt 90	rt 90
	fd 20	fd 50	fd 30
		rt 90	rt 90
		fd 100	fd 30
			rt 90
			fd 120
			rt 90
			fd 120

Page 8

You end up at square 6.

1. R U U U U U
2. U U R U U U U R R D D L
3. L L L D D D D R R D D D R

Page 11

1. U3 R3 D1
2. R3 D3 L3 U3 or D3 R3 U3 L3
3. D4 R3 U2 L3 or D2 R3 D2 L3 U2
4. U3 R3 D3 L3 or R3 U3 L3 D3
5. D1 L1 R3 L2 D3 R2 or D1 R2 L3 R1 D3 R2
6. D4 R3
7. R3 U2 L3 D3 R3 or U2 R3 D2 L3 D1 R3
8. L2 D2 L1 R2 L1 D2 L1 or L2 D2 R1 L2 R1 D2 L1
9. D1 L1 R3 L2 D3 R2 or D1 R2 L3 R1 D3 R2

Page 21

There are hundreds of ways these could be solved—here are some examples:

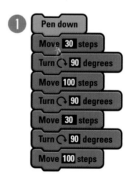

Page 13

1. forward 11
   right 90
   forward 11

2. forward 11
   right 90
   forward 11
   right 90
   forward 11
   right 90
   forward 11

3. forward 11
   left 90
   forward 11
   left 90
   forward 11
   left 90
   forward 4
   left 90
   forward 3

4. forward 11
   left 90
   forward 11
   left 90
   forward 11
   left 90
   forward 11

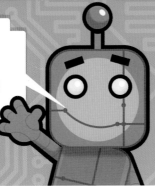

Bye for now. Happy programming!

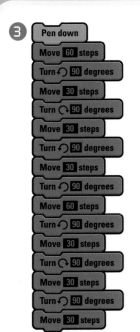

③
Pen down
Move 60 steps
Turn ↻ 90 degrees
Move 30 steps
Turn ↺ 90 degrees
Move 30 steps
Turn ↻ 90 degrees
Move 30 steps
Turn ↻ 90 degrees
Move 60 steps
Turn ↻ 90 degrees
Move 30 steps
Turn ↺ 90 degrees
Move 30 steps
Turn ↻ 90 degrees
Move 30 steps

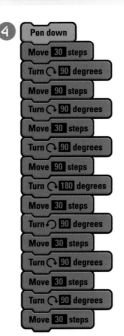

④
Pen down
Move 30 steps
Turn ↺ 90 degrees
Move 90 steps
Turn ↺ 90 degrees
Move 30 steps
Turn ↺ 90 degrees
Move 90 steps
Turn ↺ 180 degrees
Move 30 steps
Turn ↻ 90 degrees
Move 30 steps
Turn ↺ 90 degrees
Move 30 steps
Turn ↺ 90 degrees
Move 30 steps

Pages 28–29

① Get a piece of bread. Put it in the toaster. Take the toast out of the toaster. Spread butter on the toast.

② D4 R3 **U2** L3

③ fd 100
rt 90
fd 300
rt 90
fd 100
rt 90
fd **300**

④
Pen down
Move 200 steps
Turn ↻ 90 degrees
Move 200 steps
Turn ↻ 90 degrees
Move 200 steps
Turn ↻ 90 degrees
Move 200 steps

⑤
when d ▾ key pressed
point in direction 180
move 10 steps

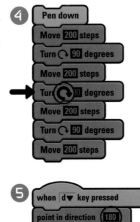

Other books in the *How to Code* series:

BOOK 2

Builds on basic coding and introduces loops and repetition. Code a maze game in Scratch and learn how to add sound effects to a game!

ISBN: 978 1 93958 189 1

BOOK 3

Take coding further by learning about selection with "if" statements. Code a simple quiz in Python or make a sandwich for a robot!

ISBN: 978 1 93958 190 7

BOOK 4

Develop your coding techniques further by learning how to create web pages using HTML. Discover how to program in JavaScript to make your pages more interactive. Build a website about pets!

ISBN: 978 1 93958 191 4

GLOSSARY

Algorithm A set of steps or rules to solve a problem.

Code A set of words or blocks that tells a computer what to do.

Command A single word or code-block that tells the computer what to do.

Data Information that can be stored and used by a computer.

Debugging Fixing problems (bugs) in a computer program.

Degree The unit of measurement for angles. If we turn all the way around, we turn 360 degrees. A quarter-turn is 90 degrees.

Download To copy data from one computer system to another, often using the internet.

Event Something that happens while a program is running, such as a key being pressed or a mouse button being clicked.

Input An action (like pressing a key) that tells a program to do something.

Language A system of words, numbers, symbols, and rules for writing programs.

Logo A computer language in which commands move a turtle around the screen to draw.

Output Something that a computer program does to show the results of a program, such as moving a sprite or making a sound.

Pixel A unit of measurement used in computing. A pixel is the smallest dot you can see on your screen.

Processor The "brain" of a computer. It carries out the instructions given by a computer program.

Program The special commands that tell a computer how to do something.

Scratch A computer language that uses blocks to make programs.

Scripts area In Scratch, this is the area to the right of the Scratch screen, where you need to drag your code blocks.

Sprite An object that moves around the screen.

Stage In Scratch, this is the area to the top left of the Scratch screen, where you can watch your sprites move around.

Turtle A robot, sprite, or arrow that can be programmed to move around the floor or the computer screen.

User The person using a program.

INDEX